FULL COLOUR

CAPTAIN UNDERPANTS
DOUBLE BOOK O' FUN

DAV PILKEY

with color by Jose Garibaldi and wes Dzioba

SCHOLASTIC

Published in the UK by Scholastic, 2022
1 London Bridge, London, SE1 9BA
Scholastic Ireland, 89E Lagan Road, Dublin Industrial Estate, Glasnevin,
Dublin, D11 HP5F

SCHOLASTIC and associated logos are trademarks and/or
registered trademarks of Scholastic Inc.

First published in the US by Scholastic Inc, 2022

Text and illustrations © Dav Pilkey, 2022
Based on content from THE CAPTAIN UNDERPANTS EXTRA-CRUNCHY BOOK O' FUN
© 2001 by Dav Pilkey, THE ALL NEW CAPTAIN UNDERPANTS EXTRA-CRUNCHY BOOK O'
FUN 2 © 2002 by Dav Pilkey

The right of Dav Pilkey to be identified
as the author and illustrator of this work has been asserted by
him under the Copyright, Designs and Patents Act 1988.

ISBN 978 0702 32521 2

A CIP catalogue record for this book is available from the British Library.

All rights reserved.
This book is sold subject to the condition that it shall not, by way of trade or
otherwise, be lent, hired out or otherwise circulated in any form of binding or
cover other than that in which it is published. No part of this publication may
be reproduced, stored in a retrieval system, or transmitted in any form or by
any other means (electronic, mechanical, photocopying, recording or otherwise)
without prior written permission of Scholastic Limited.

Printed by Bell and Bain Limited, Glasgow
Paper made from wood grown in sustainable forests and other controlled
sources.

1 3 5 7 9 10 8 6 4 2

This is a work of fiction. Names, characters, places, incidents and dialogues
are products of the author's imagination or are used fictitiously. Any
resemblance to actual people, living or dead, events or locales is entirely
coincidental.

www.scholastic.co.uk

Cover design by Dav Pilkey and Phil Falco
Book design by Dav Pilkey, Kathleen Westray, and Phil Falco
Color by Jose Garibaldi and Wes Dzioba

George and Harold's College O' Art

PAY ATTENTION NOW---This will be on The TEST!

Hi everybody. It's Time To LEARN How To make YouR Own comic BOOKS!

IT's EASY--- And FUN!!!

ALL You NEED is some PAPER, Pencils, ERASERS, AND A STAPLER.

ERASER
MR. STAPLEY

FiRST You HAVE To Think up A STORY.

And The best WAY To do THAT is To CREATE CHARACTERS.

WE'LL USE CAPTAIN UNDERPANTS AS OUR good guy.

Now we have to think up a bad guy.

How about a big, hairy toilet with werewolf fangs?

HA-HA. OK!

Now that we've got our bad guy, we need to know all about him... What powers does he have? How did he become so evil?

LASER BEAM

KUNG-FU GRIP

P.U.

Atomic Butt

Stinky Feet

NUCLEAR WASTE is often to blame for creating evil monsters. It's the comic book maker's best friend!

NEW CLEAR WASTE

NOW we need A STORY, so LeT YouR imaginATioN RuN WiLD! This REQuiReS LoTS oF __DAYDREAMING__!

DAYDREAMING is FuN, And You CAN do iT ALMOST AnywheRe--iN cLASS, oN The bus, OR even AT home!

DAYDREAMERS AT WORK! - Do NoT DISTURB!!

EDITOR'S NOTE: You really shouldn't daydream in class!

AnoTheR gReAT WAY To Think up SToRieS is cALLed "BRAINSTORMING." This is wheRe You geT TogeTheR wiTh A FRiend And LeT The ideAS __FLY__!

LeT's MAKe his ARMS And Legs ReA... So whe... FALLS...

His LASER beAMS Should be REALLY... So when CAPTAIN...

We Should make iT Like ThAT movie About The dinoSAuRS.

You meAN "TiTANiC"?

.. buT ThAT... whAT ends...

Oh YeAh! We cAN TeLL The Th...

NO! The oNe with The big T. REX!

"IT'S A WONDERFuL LiFe"?

HA-HA-H... HA-HA!!...

HA-HA HA-HA!

That's it!

Then we c... The ending chAngeS T...

Then You DRAW his FALLing!

YeAh!

RemembeR: TWO BRAINS ARE ofTen BeTTER ThAN ONE!

When You've Figured out Your story, You can START drawing Your comic. This is where TEAMWORK comes in handy. I do ALL The WRITING 'CAUSE I'm A good speller...

...And I do ALL The drawing because I'm A good ARTisT!

Don't WORRY if you make mistakes --- it happens To The best of us.

That's why They invented ERASERS.

RUB RUB RUB

Now JUST keep WRITING And drawing UnTiL you've finished Telling Your sTORy.

PROFESSOR POOPYPANTS'S
PREPOSTEROUS PUZZLES
OF PERPLEXING PERIL
PART 1

Hello kiddies! I've taken my terrifying Name Change-O-Chart 2000 and turned it into a WORD FIND PUZZLE! Try to find all the names from the chart below in the puzzle on the right. Look up, down, across, diagonal, and backward!

FIRST CHART: Use the First Letter of Your First NAME To Determine Your NEW First NAME!

A = Stinky
B = Lumpy
C = Buttercup
D = Gidget
E = Crusty
F = Greasy
G = Fluffy
H = Cheeseball
I = Funky

J = Poopsie
K = Flunky
L = Booger
M = Pinky
N = Zippy
O = Goober
P = Doofus
Q = Slimy

R = Loopy
S = Snotty
T = Falafel
U = Dorky
V = Squeezit
W = Oprah
X = Skipper
Y = Dinky
Z = Zsa-Zsa

D	Z	S	A	Z	S	A	F	L	U	N	K	Y
A	I	J	L	I	S	Q	U	E	E	Z	I	T
J	P	N	U	P	Y	S	N	O	T	T	Y	Y
A	N	C	K	P	I	N	K	Y	P	U	S	G
C	D	R	M	Y	U	H	L	I	S	A	L	O
H	Z	U	B	O	O	G	E	R	E	Y	V	O
E	L	S	K	I	P	P	E	R	B	S	F	B
E	S	T	I	N	K	Y	G	M	U	Q	A	E
S	R	Y	G	Y	Q	Y	U	F	T	D	L	R
E	O	B	P	I	F	M	O	U	T	O	A	D
B	I	O	R	F	D	O	U	T	E	R	F	W
A	O	F	U	V	D	G	E	T	R	K	E	L
L	S	L	I	M	Y	M	E	W	C	Y	L	Q
L	F	D	F	U	N	K	Y	T	U	I	O	D
O	P	R	A	H	T	P	O	O	P	S	I	E

(Answer on page 120)

HOW TO DRAW
CAPTAIN UNDERPANTS

1.

2.

3.

4.

5.

6.

7.

8.

9.

10.

11.

12.

13.

14.

15.

16.

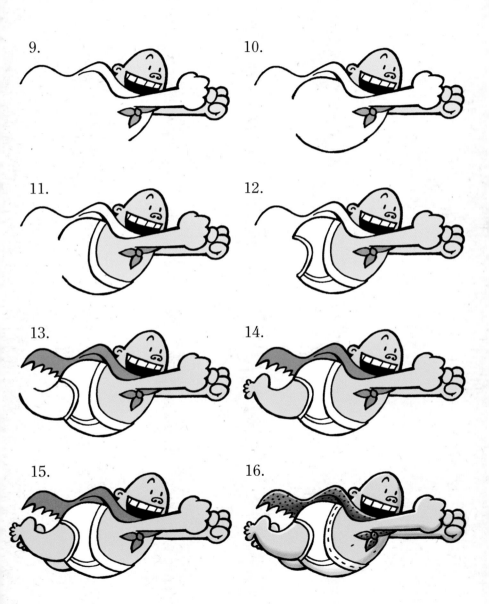

(Answer on page 120)

"Knock knock?"
"Who's there?"
"I'm a pileup."
"I'm a pileup who?"
"No, you're not! Don't be so hard on yourself, buddy!"

Q) What did the momma buffalo say to the baby buffalo when he went off to college?
A) Bison.

Q) What does lightning wear beneath its clothes?
A) Thunderwear.

Q) What should you do if you get swallowed by an elephant?
A) Jump up and down 'til you're all pooped out.

Q) Why did Batman cross his legs?
A) He had to go to the batroom.

Q) If you had fifty bananas in one hand, and twenty-five gallons of ice cream in the other, what would you have?
A) Really big hands.

THE PERILOUS PUZZLE OF PROFESSOR POOPYPANTS

ACROSS

2. The alien spacemen were named Zorx, Klax, and _____.
4. Harold's best friend is _____.
5. "George is the kid on the left with the _____ and the flat-top."
7. George's best friend is _____.
8. Don't get "weeded out" by the Deliriously Dangerous Death-Defying _____ of Doom.
10. Dr. Diaper wanted to blow up the _____.
12. Captain Underpants is also known as a principal named Mr. _____.
14. Don't get flushed by the Turbo _____ 2000!
15. "Yum, _____, eat 'em up!"

DOWN

1. "Never underestimate the power of _____."
3. _____ Horwitz Elementary School
4. Don't get blown up by the Goosy-_____ 4000.
6. Ms. Ribble is George and Harold's _____.

7. "Harold is the one on the right with the T-shirt and the bad _____."

9. Captain Underpants fights crime with Wedgie _____.

11. Professor Poopypants's first name.

13. Don't get shrunk by the Shrinky-_____ 2000.

(Answer on page 121)

HOW TO DRAW
THE TURBO TOILET 2000

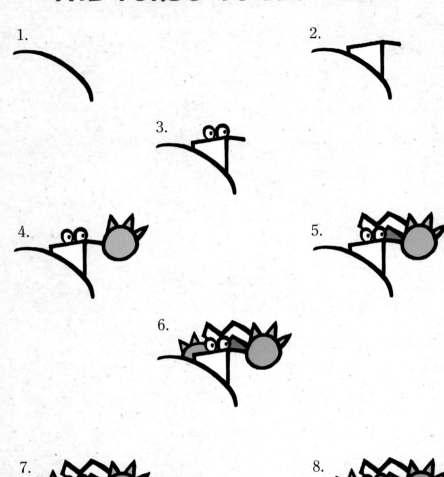

1. 2. 3. 4. 5. 6. 7. 8.

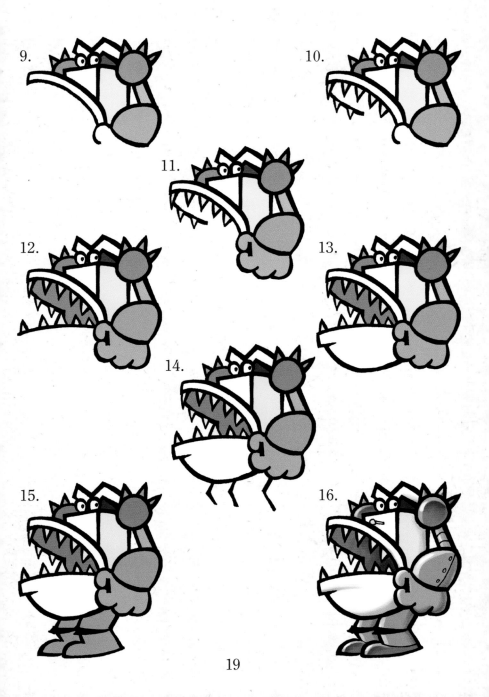

PROFESSOR POOPYPANTS'
PREPOSTEROUS PUZZLES OF PERPLEXING PERIL PART 2

So you solved my last puzzle, eh? Well, don't get too full of yourself. This puzzle is much harder! Try to find all the names from the chart below in the puzzle on the right. Look up, down, across, diagonal, and backward!

2

SECOND CHART: USE the first Letter of your Last name to determine the First half of YOUR **NEW** Last Name.

A = Diaper
B = Toilet
C = Giggle
D = Bubble
E = Girdle
F = Barf
G = Lizard
H = Waffle
I = Cootie

J = Monkey
K = Potty
L = Liver
M = Banana
N = Rhino
O = Burger
P = Hamster
Q = Toad

R = Gizzard
S = Pizza
T = Gerbil
U = Chicken
V = Pickle
W = Chuckle
X = Tofu
Y = Gorilla
Z = Stinker

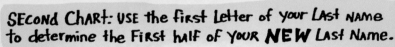

```
C  H  I  C  K  E  N  O  D  I  C  D
B  J  B  U  B  B  L  E  T  O  F  U
D  R  A  Z  Z  I  G  K  O  N  D  Q
L  G  E  X  N  O  I  T  C  C  R  B
A  I  D  T  R  M  I  O  I  U  R  I
N  G  Z  I  S  E  A  V  P  D  H  E
A  G  L  A  A  M  K  P  T  A  I  C
N  L  G  G  R  P  A  N  O  O  N  T
A  E  I  I  E  D  E  H  I  T  O  L
B  U  R  G  E  R  D  R  L  T  T  O
K  J  D  F  R  A  B  O  E  V  S  Y
G  E  L  K  C  I  P  I  T  V  V  R
G  Y  E  K  N  O  M  R  L  U  I  X
W  A  F  F  L  E  P  I  Z  Z  A  L
```

(Answer on page 121)

George And Harold's College O'Art 2

Make Your Own Flip-O-Rama!!!

Hi everybody! Today we're gonna learn how to make homemade Flip-O-Ramas!

Pay attention... This will be on the test, too!

First you need an ordinary 8½×11" piece of paper.

Got it!

Now fold the paper in half.

5½"

8½"

NOW fold the top half of your paper over the picture you've just drawn.

BECAUSE MOST PAPER IS A LITTLE TRANSPARENT, YOU SHOULD STILL KINDA BE ABLE TO SEE YOUR DRAWING UNDERNEATH.

I CAN KINDA SEE IT!

IF YOU CAN'T SEE YOUR DRAWING UNDERNEATH THE TOP SHEET OF PAPER, JUST HOLD IT UP TO A SUNNY WINDOW.

COOL!

NOW WE'RE GOING TO DO SOME TRACING ON THE TOP PAGE. THE 1ST RULE IS:
IF YOU DON'T WANT SOMETHING TO MOVE, **TRACE IT!!!**

And since he's dRibbling The bALL on the flooR, I'LL RedrAW the bALL down on the flooR.

HARoLd hAS just shown The **2ⁿᵈ** Rule of FLip-O-RAMA: If you wANt Something to move, you must **REDRAW** it iN A _New_ _position_.

 Look AT HARoLd'S Two dRAWiNgs BeLow... NoTice The differences.

FiRST dRAWiNG
(BoTTOM paGe)

secoNd dRAWiNG
(TOP PAGE)

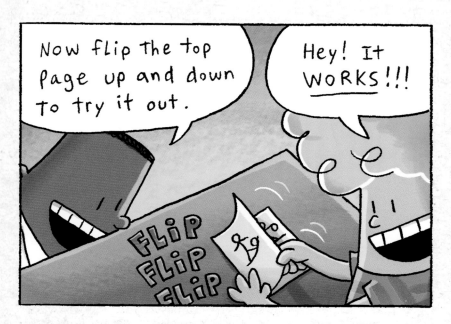

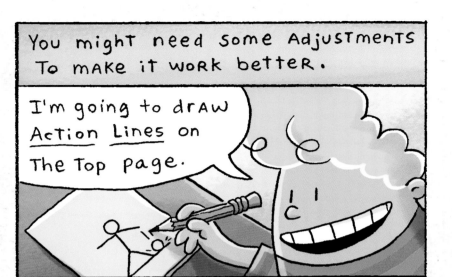

Soon you cAn move on to more exciting FLip-O-RAMAS, Like Kicks, Punches, And heAd injuries!

You'LL be A FLip-O-RAMA MASTER, with The power to AmAze And delight everyone you meet.

...WeLL, ALmost everyone!

HAPPY FLipPing

HeY Kids--- Check out the World's EASIEST FLip-O-RAMA !!!

30

Left hand Here

Right thumb Here

Right
index
FingeR
HeRe

☆ SPECIAL NOTES
FOR FLIP-O-RAMISTS

1. Typing paper and notebook paper work best.

2. Although you need to trace, don't use tracing paper. It will ruin the effect.

3. Grown-ups will freak out if your Flip-O-Ramas feature "people" beating each other up. To get around this, draw robots and monsters instead. (For some REASON, Grown-ups think that's O.K. ...Go Figure!)

4. You can get good ideas by studying the FLIP-O-RAMAS in The Captain Underpants and Dog Man Books.

Q) Why do sharks live in salt water?
A) Because pepper water makes them sneeze.

Q) How do you make a tissue dance?
A) Put a little boogie into it.

Q) Why did Tigger stick his head in the toilet?
A) He was looking for "Pooh."

Q) Who is Peter Pan's worst-smelling friend?
A) Stinkerbell.

Q) What nationality are you when you go to the bathroom?
A) European.

A woman walks into a pet store and says, "Can I get a puppy for my daughter?"
"Sorry, lady," says the pet store owner. "We don't do trades."

HOW TO DRAW
PROFESSOR POOPYPANTS

1.
2.
3.
4.
5.
6.
7.
8.
9.
10.

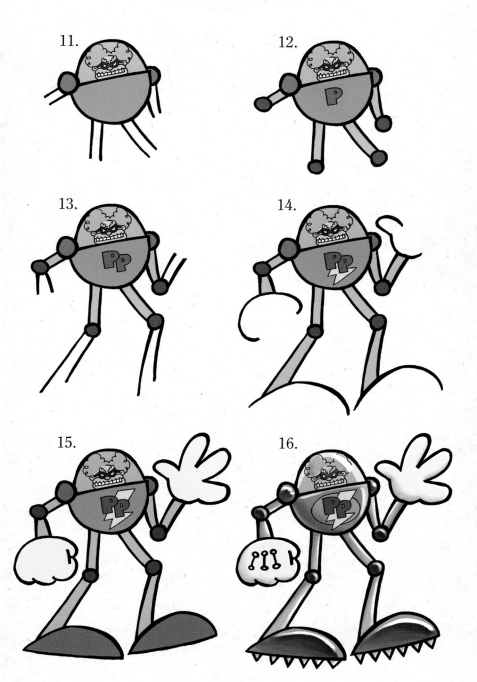

37

THE CAFETERIA LADIES' CRAZY CROSSWORD

ACROSS

1. *The Adventures of* _____ *Underpants.*
5. Mr. Krupp was transformed into a superhero by the 3-D Hypno-_____.
6. Watch out for the Equally Evil Lunchroom _____ Nerds.
8. Pippy P. Poopypants invented the _____ Jogger 2000.
10. "Hooray for Captain _____!"
11. Don't drink the Evil Zombie Nerd _____!
13. Captain Underpants often shouts "_____-La-Laaaaa!"
14. *Cheesy Animation Technology* is more commonly known as _____-O-Rama.

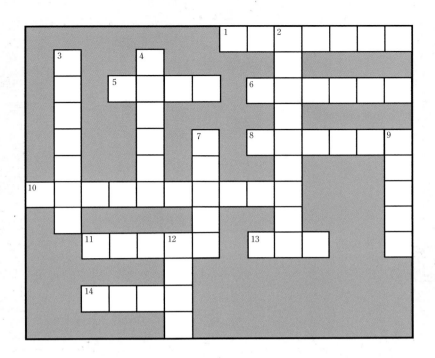

DOWN

2. *The Perilous Plot of* _____ *Poopypants.*

3. *The Attack of the* _____ *Toilets.*

4. Dr. _____ was defeated soon after George shot fake doggy doo-doo at him.

7. Zorx, Klax, and Jennifer were evil guys from outer _____.

9. A popular way to misspell the word "laughs."

12. Captain Underpants wears a red _____.

(Answer on page 121)

PROFESSOR POOPYPANTS'S PREPOSTEROUS PUZZLES OF PERPLEXING PERIL PART 3

Now comes the hardest puzzle of all. If you mess this one up, you must use the three Name Change-O-Chart 2000 charts to change your name FOREVER! Try to find all the names from the chart below in the puzzle on the right. Look up, down, across, diagonal, and backward!

Third Chart: Use The Last Letter of your Last Name To determine the Second half of your NEW Last Name.

A = Head
B = Mouth
C = Face
D = Nose
E = Tush
F = Breath
G = Pants
H = Shorts
I = Lips
J = Honker
K = Butt
L = Brain
M = Tushie
N = Chunks
O = Hiney
P = Biscuits
Q = Toes
R = Buns
S = Bottom
T = Sniffer
U = Sprinkles
V = Kisser
W = Squirt
X = Humperdinck
Y = Brains
Z = Juice

```
I  T  P  A  N  T  S  S  Y  M  S
F  Y  D  S  D  T  N  A  X  G  Z
E  G  P  A  T  U  B  R  A  I  N
J  I  E  U  B  S  H  O  R  T  S
L  H  B  N  P  H  I  N  E  Y  K
B  I  S  C  U  I  T  S  W  C  H
E  F  A  C  E  E  T  R  N  S  S
K  I  S  S  E  R  E  I  U  N  P
B  Q  E  I  I  F  D  T  I  C  R
O  O  Q  U  F  R  E  A  M  H  I
T  M  Q  I  E  Y  R  C  O  U  N
T  S  N  P  U  B  I  K  U  N  K
O  S  M  J  U  I  C  E  T  K  L
M  U  B  R  E  A  T  H  H  S  E
H  O  N  K  E  R  N  O  S  E  S
```

(Answer on page 122)

WELCOME TO A BRAND-NEW CAPTAIN UNDERPANTS STORY . . . AND YOU'RE THE STAR!

Before you read the story on the following pages, go through and find all the blanks. Below each blank is a small description of what you need to write in the blank. Just fill in the blank with an appropriate word.

For example, if the blank looks like this:

_____ , you would think up an adjective
(an adjective)

and put it in the blank like this: _____ Stinky _____ .
(an adjective)

Remember, don't read the story first. It's more fun if you go through and fill in the blanks first, THEN read the story.

When you're done, follow the instructions at the bottom of each page to complete the illustrations. Cool, huh?

JUST FOR REMINDERS:
A **verb** is an action word (like jump, swim, kick, squish, run, etc.).
An **adjective** is a word that describes a person, place, or thing (lumpy, purple, hairy, etc.).

CAPTAIN UNDERPANTS VS. THE EVIL MONSTER
(STARRING GEORGE, HAROLD, AND YOU!)

Once upon a time, George, Harold, and their

friend _____ were busy studying
             (your name)

about the wonders of _____
                         (an adjective)

_____ , when their new science
   (disgusting things)

teacher, Mr. _____ , accidentally
             (a funny name)

spilled some _____ _____
          (a gross adjective)   (a liquid)

on a pile of toxic _____ .
                 (silly things)

(Draw yourself sitting here.)

(Draw the teacher spilling liquid onto some toxic stuff.)

Suddenly, the pile began to morph into

a giant, evil _____ .
(a silly thing)

"Help," cried _____ , "a
(somebody in your class)

giant, evil _____
(the silly thing you just used above)

just stepped on my lunchbox and ate up

_____ !"
(your gym teacher's name)

"Oh, NO!" cried Mr. Krupp. "The poor

lunchbox!"

↑
(Draw the giant,
evil monster.)

↖
(Draw the kid
in your class.)

George, Harold, and _____
(your name)

tried to escape by hiding behind a

_____ . Then _____
(a very small thing)   (your name)

snapped _____ fingers.
(his/her/their/etc.)

Soon, a _____ grin came
(an adjective)

across Mr. Krupp's face as he dropped

his _____ _____
(an adjective)   (an article of clothing)

and ran to his office.

↑
(Draw
yourself.)

↑
(Draw the thing you're
hiding behind.)

↖
(Draw the giant,
evil monster.)

Soon, Captain Underpants

_____ through the
(an action verb ending in "ed")

wall. He grabbed a _____
(an adjective)

_____ and hit the monster
(a thing)

on its _____ .
(a body part)

"Ouchies!" screamed the monster. It

turned and _____
(a fight move ending in "ed")

Captain Underpants on his

_____ .
(a body part)

(Draw
yourself.)

(Draw the monster fighting
Captain Underpants.)

_____ quickly mixed up a bottle
(your name)

of _____ with a jar of toxic,
(something a kid would drink)

_____ _____ .
(an adjective)   (disgusting things)

"Hey, _____ ," said George,
(your name)

"where'd you find that jar of crazy stuff?!!?"

"It was right here next to this barrel of

toxic _____ _____ ," said
(an adjective)   (different disgusting things)

_____ .
(your name)

"Oh," said Harold. "That makes sense."

↑
(Draw yourself creating
a strange mixture.)

↑
(Complete the label
on the barrel.)

_____ shook up the strange

(your name)

mixture and threw it at the monster.

"_____ !" screamed

(something you might scream or cheer)

the monster as it fell over and died

of a massive _____ attack.

(a body part)

"That makes sense, too," said George.

Unfortunately, some of the mixture

splashed on Captain Underpants's head,

and he turned back into Mr. Krupp.

(Draw yourself throwing the strange
concoction onto the monster.)

(Draw the monster
getting splashed.)

48

"HOLY _____ _____ !"
(an adjective)   (silly animals)

shouted Mr. Krupp. "I'll bet that George,

Harold, and _____ are responsible
(your name)

for this mess!" So he punished the three kids

by making them _____ in the
(an action verb)

_____ for _____ hours.
(a room in the school)   (a number)

"This has got to be the dumbest story

we've ever been in," said George.

"Don't blame me," said Harold. "_____
(your name)

wrote it!"

↑
(Draw yourself
looking guilty.)

ZORX, KLAX, AND Jennifer's Big, Bad BATCH OF Zombie NERD Juice

(Answer on page 122)

FINAL EXAM

Hi everybody!

One thing I know for sure is that kids LOVE to study and take tests! That's why we've included this incredibly difficult FINAL EXAM! Make sure you've studied BOTH of George and Harold's College o' Art comics. When you think you're ready, take out a pencil, turn the page, and begin.

Good Luck!

1. What's the BEST way to think up a story?
a) Create characters.
b) Put a grilled cheese sandwich on your head.
c) Roll around in steak sauce, then bark like a dog.

2. What is often to blame for creating monsters?
a) society
b) pep rallies
c) nuclear waste

3. What two things also help you think up stories?
a) brainstorming and daydreaming
b) braindreaming and daystorming
c) daybraining and dreamstorming

4. Don't worry about making mistakes. That's why they invented _____.
a) lawyers
b) erasers
c) soap-on-a-rope

5. If you have trouble writing action scenes, you can always use _____.
a) a ghost writer
b) Flip-O-Rama
c) egg salad

6. When making comics, be prepared to:
a) win friends and influence people
b) smell like Cheez Whiz™
c) suffer for your art

7. What's the world's EASIEST Flip-O-Rama?

a) a guy with a chicken up his nose

b) a guy with a basketball

c) a guy with a basketball up his nose

8. The FIRST rule of Flip-O-Rama is: If you don't want something to move, _____.

a) trace it

b) put it in a "time-out"

c) threaten to stop the car

9. The SECOND rule of Flip-O-Rama is: If you want something to move, you must _____.

a) make rude noises with your armpits

b) drink lots of prune juice

c) redraw it in a new position

10. The more you practice, _____.

a) the better you get

b) the worse you get

c) the stinkier you get

Now put your pencil down, and let's see how you did.

ANSWERS:
1: a, 2: c (though technically "b" is also correct),
3: a, 4: b, 5: b, 6: c, 7: b, 8: a, 9: c, 10: a

If you got at least 6 right, CONGRATULATIONS! You've just graduated from George and Harold's College o' Art.

(Answer on page 123)

Hairy Potty

AND the

UNDERWEAR OF JUSTICE

BY G. R. BEARD and H.M. Hutchins

Once upon a time There was a scientist who worked At "Hair Group for Guys."

He was trying To invent a Hair Growth Formula.

Hmmm.

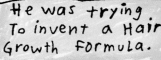

But it didn't work.

Fooey!

Then he tried Adding **NUCLEAR WASTE** To his concoction.

The SCIENTIST tried his New FormuLA on A frog.

RiBBit.

The frog grew HAir...

Hooray!

The frog grew **Big**...

Uh-oh!

The FROG grew EviL!

ROAR!

mommy!

Fortunately, the scientist HAd A cAN of "FROG-AWAY" BrAnd Frog Remover in his LAB.

ROAR!

FROG AWAY FROG REMOV

FroG AWAY FroG AWAY

MAKES Frogs CROAK!

The scientist decided to get rid of the bad formula so that nothing else would grow big and hairy and evil.

So he poured it down the toilet.

BUT---He forgot to FLUSH!

Soon, the toilet grew hair.

Then the toilet grew BIG.

Then the toilet grew evil!

The scientist Reached FOR A can of "POTTY-BE-GONE" Brand Toilet Remover...

...but the box WAS empty!

POTTY-BE-GONE
TOILET REMOVER
Time TO RE-ORDER
TERMINATE YOUR TOILET!

GULP.

The HAIRY Potty shot a LASER BEAM From his Mouth And **ZAPPED** the scientist.

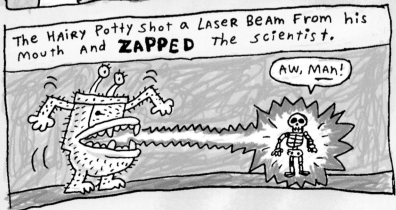

AW, MAN!

Hairy Potty shot his laser and made a hole in the wall.

ZAP

I'm free!!!

Then he ran around causing mischief.

BOB'S DINER
AT BOB'S DINER, YOU'LL FIND THAT WE PICK THE BEST INGREDIENTS. YOUR NOSE **KNOWS** THE DIFFERENCE!

Hmmm.

ZAP

BOB'S
AT BOB'S DINER, WE PICK YOUR NOSE

HAW HAW HAW

Then Hairy Potty ran to a school.

LA-LA LA-LA.

62

To be continued . . .

WEDGIE-POWERED WORD FIND

Try to find the names below in the puzzle on the right. Look up, down, backward, and diagonally.

CHARACTER NAME BONUS QUIZ:
How well do you know your UNDERPANTS?

Draw lines from the <u>first</u> names in Chart A to the matching <u>last</u> names in Chart B.

CHART A	CHART B
Benny	Beard
Billy	Fyde
George	Hoskins
Harold	Hutchins
Melvin	Krupp
Morty	Poopypants
Pippy	Ribble
Tara	Sneedly
Tippy	Tinkletrousers

S	T	N	A	P	Y	P	O	O	P
R	U	O	R	L	Y	H	Q	N	A
E	G	N	L	V	X	T	V	F	F
S	N	I	H	C	T	U	H	L	Z
U	B	V	M	A	L	O	E	S	A
O	A	L	F	O	S	G	D	R	J
R	U	E	C	K	R	R	A	Q	E
T	F	M	I	O	A	T	D	D	I
E	S	N	E	E	D	L	Y	V	E
L	S	G	B	L	O	F	L	R	S
K	Q	F	F	R	B	P	C	P	U
N	S	E	A	E	R	B	I	C	R
I	A	H	N	Y	P	P	I	T	Z
T	X	N	M	J	P	P	U	R	K
K	Y	Q	B	Y	R	Z	X	D	C

(Answers on page 123)

HOW TO DRAW
CAPTAIN UNDERPANTS

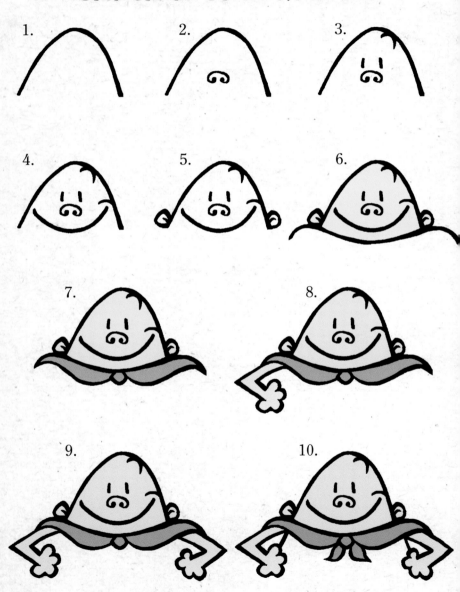

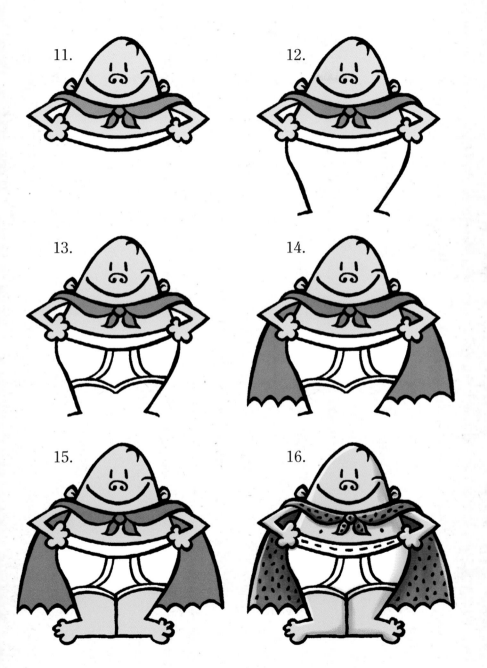

PERPLEXING PEEWEE-POWERED PUZZLE

ACROSS

3. Captain Underpants fights for Truth, Justice, and all that is Pre-Shrunk and _____!

5. A flushable porcelain bowl.

7. "Tra-_____-Laaaaa!"

8. Super Diaper Baby's archenemy is _____ Doo-Doo.

9. Captain Underpants is nicknamed the _____ Warrior.

10. Super Diaper Baby's best friend is Diaper _____.

11. The only five-letter word (starting with an "s") to appear twice in the last six clues.

14. Watch out for the Wicked Wedgie _____!

15. Liquid spray _____ is the enemy of underwear.

DOWN

1. The three evil space guys were named _____, Klax, and Jennifer.

2. New Swissland's most famous scientist is Professor _____.

3. Three cheers for _____ Underpants!

4. _____ Potty and the Underwear of Justice.

6. Beware of the _____ Toilet 2000!

10. Billy Hoskins is better known as Super _____ Baby.

12. Don't spill the Extra-Strength Super _____ Juice!

13. Ms. _____ turned into the Wicked Wedgie Woman.

(Answer on page 124)

HOW TO DRAW
MR. KRUPP

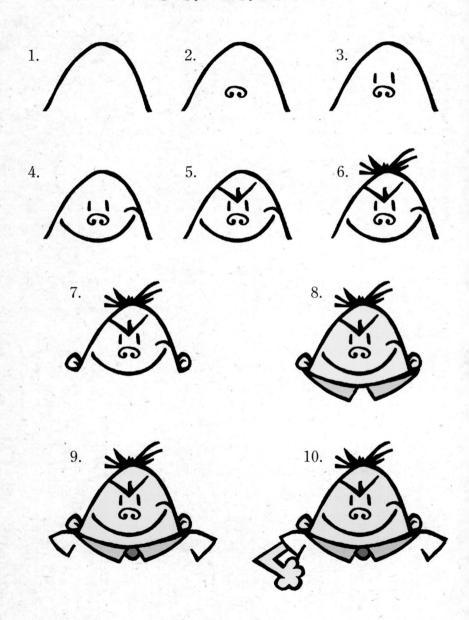

HeLP George and Harold Get into Their Tree House

(Answer on page 125)

Q) Why did the cookie cry?
A) Because his mom had been a wafer so long.

"Knock knock."
"Who's there?"
"Olive Toop."
"Olive Toop who?"
"Well, so do I, but you don't hear me braggin' about it!"

Ms. Ribble: Harold, if I gave you two goldfish, and Melvin gave you four goldfish, how many would you have?
Harold: Eleven.
Ms. Ribble: ELEVEN?!!? Hah! You're WRONG, bub!
Harold: No, you're wrong. I already have five goldfish back at home!

Melvin: Excuse me, mister, I'd like to buy some toilet paper.
Grocery store clerk: What color would you like?
Melvin: Just give me white. I'll color it myself!

Q) What do you get when you cross a porcupine with a great white shark?
A) As far away as possible.

HOW TO DRAW
GEORGE

1.

2.

3.

4.

5.

6.

7.

8.

9.

10.

11.

12.

13.

14.

15.

16.

HOW TO DRAW
HAROLD

1.

2.

3.

4.

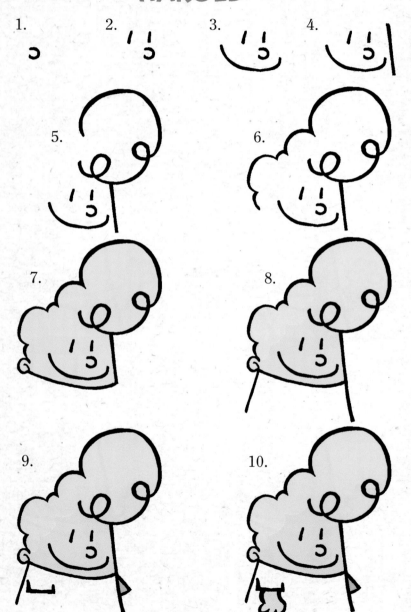

5.

6.

7.

8.

9.

10.

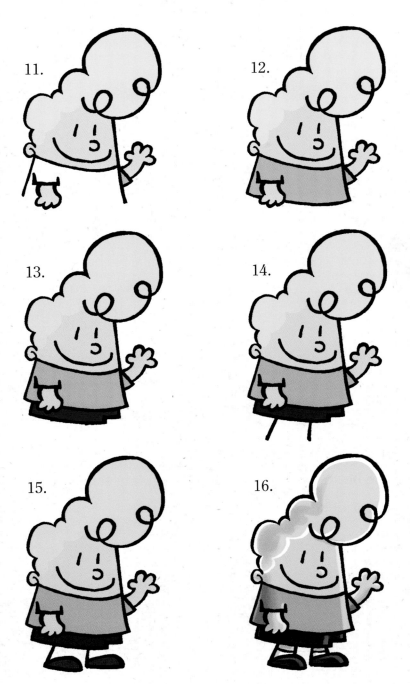

NOW YOU CAN BE THE STAR OF YOUR OWN SUPER-CHEESY CAPTAIN UNDERPANTS STORY!

Before you read the story on the following pages, go through and find all the blanks. Below each blank is a small description of what you need to write in the blank. Just fill in the blank with an appropriate word.

For example, if the blank looks like this:

_____ , you would think up an adjective
(an adjective)
and put it in the blank like this: _____ Snotty _____ .
(an adjective)

Remember, don't read the story first. It's more fun if you go through and fill in the blanks first, THEN read the story.

When you're done, follow the instructions at the bottom of each page to complete the illustrations. Cool, huh?

JUST FOR REMINDERS:
A **verb** is an <u>action</u> word (like jump, swim, kick, squish, run, etc.).
An **adjective** is a word that <u>describes</u> a person, place, or thing
(lumpy, purple, hairy, etc.).

THE INCREDIBLY STUPID ADVENTURE OF CAPTAIN UNDERPANTS

This is George Beard, Harold Hutchins,

and _____ _____ .
　　　　(your first name)　　　　(your last name)

George is the one on the left with the tie and

the flat-top. Harold is the one on the right

with the T-shirt and the bad haircut.

_____ is the one in the middle
　(your first name)

with the _____ _____
　　　　　(an adjective)　　　　(article of clothing)

and the _____ _____ .
　　　　　(an adjective)　　　　(body part or parts)

Remember that now.

↑
(Draw yourself here.)

One day, George, Harold, and _____
(your first name)
were at school when suddenly, an evil, _____
(an adjective)
villain _____ through the door and
(a verb ending in "ed")
roared like a ferocious _____ .
(a harmless insect)

"My name is Commander _____
(a gross adjective)
_____ !" shouted the villain. "And I've come
(a gross thing)
to destroy all the _____ in the world!"
(smelly things)

Commander _____
(the gross adjective and thing you used above)
grabbed a _____ and started hitting
(a piece of furniture)
_____ on the _____ with it.
(your gym teacher's name)   (a body part)

"Oh no!" cried _____ . "That villain is
(your first name)
going to hurt the poor _____ !"
(the piece of furniture you used above)

(Draw yourself here.)   (Draw your evil villain here.)

"We've got to stop that monster!" cried

George. He reached into his _____ ,
(an article of clothing)
grabbed a/an _____ _____ ,
(an adjective)   (something big)
and threw it at the villain.

Harold found a/an _____ in his
(something bigger)
_____ , so he threw that, too. Finally,
(an article of clothing)
_____ reached into his/her/their_____ ,
(your name)   (an article of clothing)
pulled out a/an _____ _____ ,
(an adjective)   (the biggest thing you can think of)
and threw that as well.

But nothing seemed to stop the _____
(a disgusting adjective)
Commander _____ !
(the gross adjective and thing you used twice on page 80)

(Draw yourself here.)   (Draw the stuff you are   (Draw your evil
                                throwing through the air.)   villain here.)

"This looks like a job for Captain Underpants!"

shouted _____ .
　　　　　　(your first name)

　　Suddenly, Captain Underpants _____
　　　　　　　　　　　　　　　　　(a verb ending in "ed")

into the school. "Hi," said Captain Underpants.

"How's your _____ _____
　　　　　　　(an adjective)　　　　(an animal)

_____ today?"
(a part of the body)

　　"That doesn't make any sense," said Harold.

　　"Who cares?" said _____ . "We've got
　　　　　　　　　　　　(your first name)

to stop that villain!" So Captain Underpants

grabbed a baseball bat and hit Commander

_____ over the
(the gross adjective and thing you used twice on page 80)

head repeatedly.

(Draw yourself here.)　　　　　(Draw your evil villain here.)

HERE COMES THE BAT, MAN!

(Draw your villain here. Make him about the same height
as Captain Underpants. If you need help, look at the
Flip-O-Ramas on pages 31 and 33 for inspiration.)

HERE COMES THE BAT, MAN!

(Draw your villain here. Make him about the same height
as Captain Underpants. If you need help, look at the
Flip-O-Ramas on pages 31 and 33 for inspiration.)

"Holy _____ _____ !" shouted
(a verb ending in "ing")　　　(an animal)

George. "Captain Underpants has defeated

Commander _____!"
(the gross adjective and thing you used twice on page 80)

"Let's celebrate by eating _____ servings of
(a number)

_____ _____ and drinking _____ cups
(an adjective)　　(something gross)　　　　　　　　(a number)

of _____ _____ ," said Harold.
(an adjective)　　(a disgusting liquid)

"That sounds delicious," said _____ .
(your first name)

"Just be sure to sprinkle some _____
(a gross adjective)

_____ on my food, and add a slice of
(creepy things)

_____ to my _____ ."
(something gross)　　(the disgusting liquid you used above)

(Draw yourself sitting here.)　　(Draw your defeated villain lying here

86

(Answer on page 125)

HOW TO DRAW
WEDGIE WOMAN

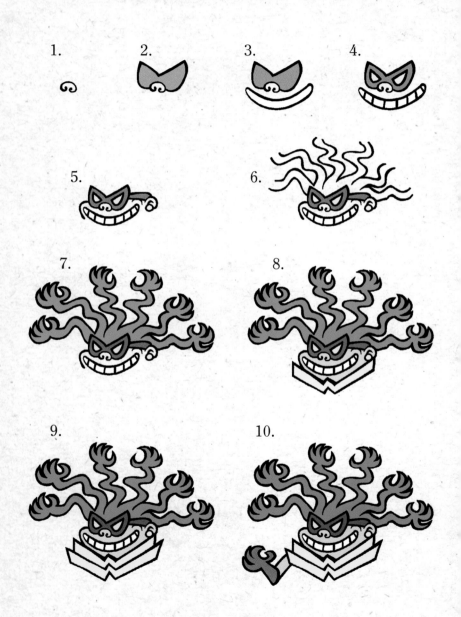

1.
2.
3.
4.
5.
6.
7.
8.
9.
10.

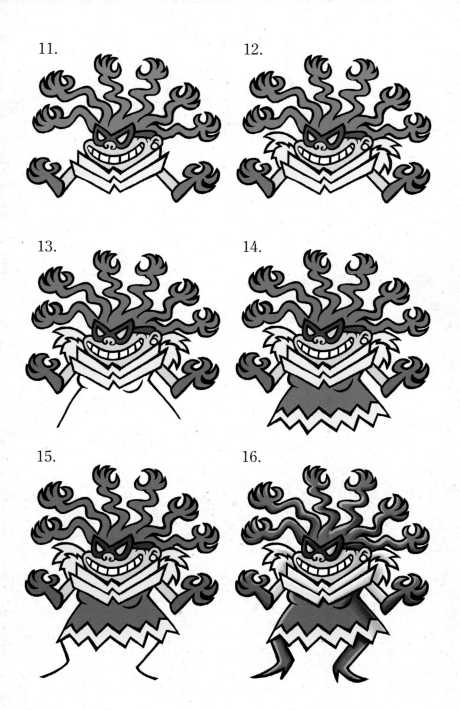

HOW TO DRAW
ZORX, KLAX, AND JENNIFER

1.

2.

3.

4.

5.

6.

7.

8.

9.

10.

FUN WITH
ACCESSORIES

1. Add eyelashes!

2. Add lipstick!

3. Add a bow!

4a.

4b.

ZORXETTE

5a.

5b.

KLAXETTE

6a.

6b.

JENNIFERETTE

92

Get ready for the
spine-tingling conclusion of

Hairy Potty

AND the

UNDERWEAR OF JUSTICE

BY G. R. BEARD and H. M. Hutchins

TreeHouse Comix

INCORPORATED

HAIRY POTTY chased OUR Hero outside.

HEYMON'S GIFTS
Who makes the CUTEST Gifts And the Most delicious Cheese? ...WE DO!

ZAP

HEY Who CUT the Cheese?

CAPTAIN UNDERPANTS WAS Faster Than A speeding Waistband...

ZAP!
zip

... MORE POWER-FuL Than BOXER SHORTS...

TRIP

94

... And ABLE to LEAP TALL Buildings WiTHOUT getting A Wedgie.

TRA·LA·LAAAAA!

ZAP

BONK

But HAiRY PoTTY WAS PoWERFuL, too. He Shot An EViL LASER Beam at Captain UnderpanTs.

ZAAP

Hey! what's going on here? How come You're not dead?

NEVER UNDER-ESTIMATE The Power of UNDERWEAR!

95

Finally, CAPTAIN UNDERPANTS AND HAiry Potty got into A Big, Terrible FighT.

WARNiNG

The Following FighT CoNTAiNS very GraPHic violence.

PLease cover your eyes when you TuRN The pages OR you might get explosive Diarrhea.

—Thank You

FLiP·O·RAMA

HERE's HOW it WORKS !!!!

STEP 1

Place your Left Hand inside the dotted Lines marked "LEFT HAND Here." Hold the BOOK open FLAT.

STEP 2

GRASP the Right-hand page with your Right Thumb and index Finger (inside the dotted Lines marked "Right THUMB HERE").

STEP 3

Now Quickly Flip The Right-hand page back and Forth until the picture apears to be animated.

(For extra fun, try adding your own Sound-effects!)

FLIP-O-RAMA #1
(Pages 99 And 101)

Remember, flip <u>only</u> page 99. While you are flipping, be sure you can See the picture on page 99 <u>And</u> the one on page 101.

If you flip Quickly, the two pictures will Start to Look Like <u>One</u> Animated picture.

Left Hand Here

The EyeBall Basher

RIGHT
Thumb
Here

Right
index
Finger
Here

The EyeBall Basher

FLIP-O-RAMA #2

(pages 103 and 105)

Remember, flip only page 103. While you are flipping, be sure you can see the picture on page 103 And the one on page 105.

If you flip Quickly, the two pictures will start to look like One Animated picture.

Left Hand Here

THE KOO-KOO CLAP

RIGHT
Thumb
Here

Right
index
Finger
Here

THE KOO-KOO CLAP

FLIP-O-RAMA #3

(pages 107 and 109)

Remember, flip <u>only</u> page 107. While you are flipping, be sure you can see the picture on page 107 <u>And</u> the one on page 109.

If you flip Quickly, the two pictures will Start to Look Like <u>One</u> Animated Picture.

Left Hand Here

The Potty Pounder

RIGHT thumb Here

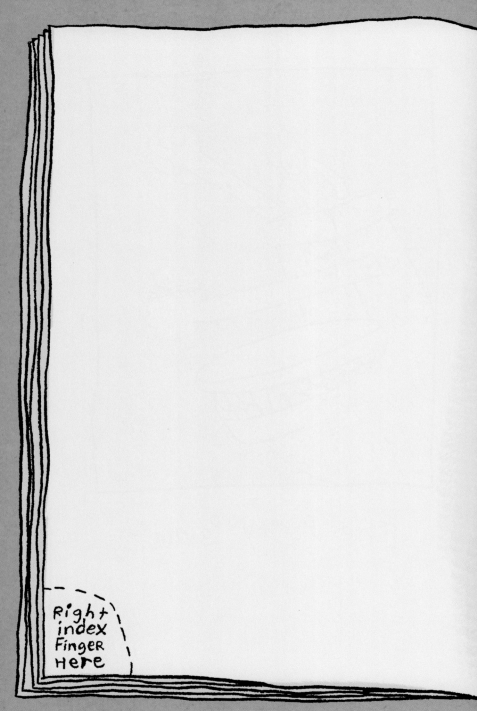

Right index Finger Here

The Potty Pounder

FLIP·O·RAMA # 4

(pages 111 and 113)

Remember, flip _only_ page 111.
While you are flipping, be sure
you can see the picture on
page _111_ _And_ the one on
page 113.

If you flip Quickly,
the two pictures will
start to look like
One Animated picture.

Left Hand
Here

The Psycho Stomp

RIGHT
Thumb
Here

Right
index
Finger
Here

The Psycho Stomp

118

ANSWERS

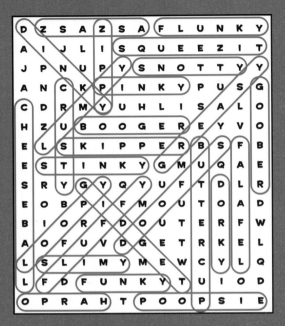

Word Find
page 11

Maze
page 14

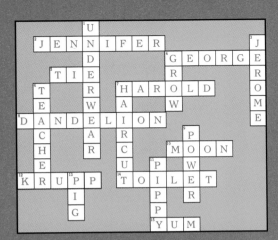

Crossword
page 17

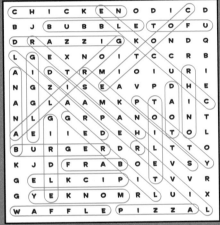

Word Find
page 21

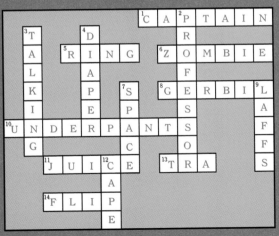

Crossword
page 39

121

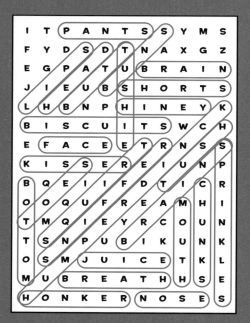

Word Find
page 41

Maze
page 50

Maze
page 55

Bonus Quiz
page 64

CHART A	CHART B
Benny	Beard
Billy	Fyde
George	Hoskins
Harold	Hutchins
Melvin	Krupp
Morty	Poopypants
Pippy	Ribble
Tara	Sneedly
Tippy	Tinkletrousers

Word Find
page 65

Crossword
page 69

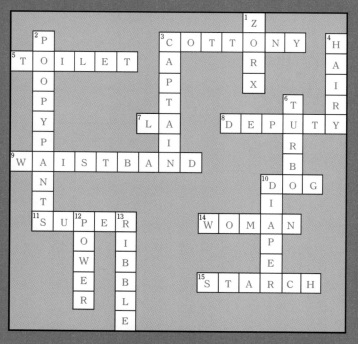

Across

5. TOILET
3. COTTONY
7. LA
8. DEPUTY
9. WAISTBAND
10. DOG
11. SUPER
14. WOMAN
15. STARCH

Down

1. Z...
2. POPPYPANT...
3. CAPTAI...
4. HAIRR...
6. TRB...
12. POWER
13. RIBBLE

Maze
page 72

Maze
page 87

GET READING W

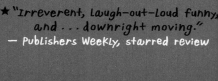

★ "Irreverent, laugh-out-loud funny,
and . . . downright moving."
— Publishers Weekly, starred review

ABOUT THE
AUTHOR-ILLUSTRATOR

When Dav Pilkey was a kid, he was diagnosed with ADHD and dyslexia. Dav was so disruptive in class that his teachers made him sit out in the hallway every day. Luckily, Dav loved to draw and make up stories. He spent his time in the hallway creating his own original comic books — the very first adventures of Dog Man and Captain Underpants.

In college, Dav met a teacher who encouraged him to write and illustrate for kids. He took her advice and created his first book, WORLD WAR WON, which won a national competition in 1986. Dav made many other books before being awarded the California Young Reader Medal for DOG BREATH (1994) and the Caldecott Honor for THE PAPERBOY (1996).

In 2002, Dav published his first full-length graphic novel for kids, called THE ADVENTURES OF SUPER DIAPER BABY. It was both a USA Today and New York Times bestseller. Since then, he has published more than a dozen full-length graphic novels for kids, including the bestselling Dog Man and Cat Kid Comic Club series.

Dav's stories are semi-autobiographical and explore universal themes that celebrate friendship, empathy, and the triumph of the good-hearted.

When he is not making books for kids, Dav loves to kayak with his wife in the Pacific Northwest.

Learn more at Pilkey.com.